STRANGE QUESTIONS TO ASK LIBRARIANS

STRANGE QUESTIONS TO ASK LIBRARIANS

A Poetry Collection

KAITLYN BOLYARD

Blind Goose Publishing

CONTENTS

To all the wonderful librarians I have known over the years

Here, Together

As winter arrives, we talk in movie quotes,
Push aside our cats gathering at the front windows,
So we can behold the snow swiftly falling.

We brew coffee and forget, standing half-naked in the kitchen,
Reading travel blogs about Greenland.
Our marriage, at eight years, still lingers, still persists.

We imagine traveling could save us,
If we could just escape the boundaries of our home,
Embrace our bodies, stretched out, feeling alone.

We have grown old enough to no longer care
How we hold each other (or don't), but
Here, together, we still

Test positive for COVID.

No Place

January 18, 2022

As I walk through fast-growing fields,
I count each day breaking across the horizon.
Out here, in the wide-open sky,
I count each row of wheat, reminding me
Of work still left to be done.

Following the coast full of surf and sand,
My steps grow slow, my ears crashing with waves.
I edge onto a slick rock, staring out at the place
Where water meets sky, unable to discern
Heaven from earth, and yet I try.

When night closes in, heavy with memory,
I retreat to the woods, great pines towering over me,
Holding me close with needled branches,
A sharp, painful embrace. There seems to be
No place for me to escape.

What it Means to be Real

January 20, 2022

I feel invisible when we stand in line,
Just a shadow of the other students.
After class, my teachers drink and laugh but never remember me.

I never understood why my mom lies,
Pretends to be normal, says I'm normal too,
When all I want is to run and hide somewhere far, far away.

I steal money from her piggy bank and throw rocks
Ricocheting off the riverbank, unable to calm
The anger bubbling up under my skin, my only skin.

For all those fantasy worlds I've read about,
Your time has come; open for me a doorway,
A way to escape from this place; I'd rather cry alone

Over fictional characters, who treat me like I'm human,
More real than any adult I've ever known.

Splitting An Opinion

January 25, 2022

He plagiarized himself, a night owl caught in his own shadow,
Writing notes on his own genius.
His sixteen-year-old self considered his machinations musical,
Decided he could wait for the bathroom but still felt friendless,
Undervalued and overworked.
He could only recommend one alternative perspective at the next meeting.
His viewpoints made it more difficult to decide, to vote for the right candidate,
To speak words of endearment without crying.
After Monday, he walked the dog and dragged muddy pawprints the length of a fancy rug.
By Wednesday and Thursday, he was sampling whiskey, speaking straight facts.
He received a package larger than Bukowski's if we're measuring.
He disliked poets and warm fragrances and thought he could split his opinion
Fifty-fifty by supporting Carhart but refusing the vaccine.

Completed Puzzles

We take the space of our Saturday off,
Fluff, groom, and fill it with errands.
So that by the time we scratch off each item
On our to-do lists, we feel too tired to enjoy
Venturing above ground amongst humans.

We try to stay social online during these
Trying times. We remember cousins who
Used to visit, spreading itchy chicken pox soars
Like they were something a child wanted.
Now we just sit, trapped with our dust.

We take showers so hot our skin melts off,
Just trying to feel clean for once, to free ourselves
From anxiety. We wish we could be
Worshipped like serial killers, gain notoriety,
Celebrating the completed puzzles of our lives
Each piece fitting together perfectly.

For the Rest of the Winter

January 30, 2022

I want to streak through this winter wind,
Bare my limbs to the cold slap of it,
Until death feels imminent.
I tried dying once, but you'll have to take my word for it,
Forgot to share on social media, felt too exhausted, too limited.

I want to share this moment with our unborn son, the one
We'll name Zeus against your wishes. I wish you could feel excited about this.
I know you have goals, but they pale compared to mine.
All I have left to offer is what's left of me.

I no longer own the watch you gave to me,
Can't remember who owned it before me,
Because I smashed its face when time argued,
Took your love and trashed it.

Which religion got it right when they realized
None of us go anywhere after we die?
Just fall back into the void, never-ending.

I need to stop bumping into ideas, stubbing my brain
The way I bruise myself just trying to navigate furniture.
This will be me for the rest of the winter, overthinking,
Going on mini-adventures through stream-of-consciousness writing

Standing in the doorway, letting warm air out as I stare at the snow.

Before Real Life Begins, We Read

January 31, 2022

I wish I could remember my memories,
Write more cohesive poetry,
Learn to feel proud of my buying power.

Books have been helping us avoid conversation
Since 1454 and we keep writing more of them,
Delving into fantasy worlds, sex dreams,
Inspecting the cobwebs at the back of our minds,
Carefully counting each year wasted.

Sometimes students actually visit during office hours,
Sometimes adult friendships feel easy,
But first, we open a book and lose ourselves completely.
Sometimes the hammer hits the nail on the head rather than my thumb,
Sometimes I play outside in zero-degree weather,
Fight sparkly bitches with a dagger for my love.

I finally finished a life-size masterpiece, reached my childhood goals,
Met an online class with heavy weightiness.
Great research resources help me launch my writing legacy,
Chop down the world's last beanstalk and orphan giants.

Living people might eat dead mushrooms, but living mushrooms
Munch on our ancestors. Despite this,
We continue to learn and grow,
Subscribe to the algorithm of social media's flow.

Reading About My Life

February 2, 2022

I am an anarchy harpy,
Flying through membranous dreams,
A female mind tricking itself to sleep.
I will live my whole life freaked out,
Boarding the plane with white knucks, but I know
I can live through anything, for I am strong.

As a kid, I watched a spear of asparagus
Singing about Christian values,
But none of it sunk in.
I remain absolutely, stunningly convinced
Bigfoot is just a misunderstood ape,
Who should prize fight King Kong.

Meanwhile, in an alternate universe,
I exist in an awkward bookworm moment,
Casually reading about my own life,
Examining it from a distance,
Knowing everything people think of me is wrong.

Strange Questions to Ask Librarians

February 1, 2022

What identity issues define who you are as a person?
On the first day of the Spring semester, were your elbow patches
Brown or grey or covered in sequins?
Can you portray a tough alpha leader, or do you follow the pack?
If you pulled up your ancestry, how far can you go back,
And what level of privilege has allowed you to keep track?
What is "normal," whatever that means?
How much mashed potatoes can you eat?
If a child wore blackface to kindergarten, who faces punishment?
What do you understand but still perceive as magic?
In forty days, the sun will set at seven, and the frosty months
Will end – how will you celebrate?

Weirdos drinking white Ukrainians

March 12, 2022

The last author on the planet sold $11 mantras,
Only available to Chicago residents with adopted dogs.
If you check out her book, you'll still be chilled,
But forget how much you hate people at work.

There is a race for every type of runner here, but I,
I'll be damned if I'm going back where I've been; sorry I didn't unfriend
Your abuser sooner.

Nothing is impossible except deciding where to eat.
We could drink fresh mozzarella juice like boba tea.
Did you know sea cucumbers have anal teeth?
These wildly inventive fragrances have gotten me through my first few
seasons,
But I need proof of why we're still so weird.

Order a white Ukrainian instead of a white Russian,
And we'll skydive naked into the Kremlin with our guitars and guns.

Hot-off-the-wire Desire

March 20, 2022

Let us celebrate fertility with a joyous Ostara,
Excitement building before the big event.
But a 20 on the die still doesn't hit the target,
Doesn't even step into the entryway.
Some people slip by silent, pretending the sheets
Spread into a warm private beach, comfortable nudity.
I feel your every response, every intake of breath,
A bridge between your chest and mine
But I can't reap the building heat.
Shiver, instead, unsure of the hydration I need.
A greedy villain between my legs demands more,
Needs you to speak another language here,
Needs you to articulate your feelings before
Hot-off-the-wire desire can turn red in silhouette,
Proudly muddying our relationship.

Carrying My Heart

March 21, 2022

As a child, my brother verbally attacked our parents
For still feeling young at forty.
Every Sunday, he would read at least 90% of the obituaries,
Scanning carefully for their names.
He invented scorpion and cheese pizza and earned
A pirate certificate, as well as publishing rights
For a patented high-waisted fit called Sharpay.
He favored more afternoon sunlight and made
Every weekend last at least three days.
He made interesting points about sexism
From the comfort of his own home and celebrated Poetry Day
By sharing hard-copy media with commentary tracks.
He is a Wiccan who hails Eris when it rains.
He has always carried my heart with him,
Still beating, still bloody,
Wrapped in a crumpled paper bag.

Welcome to the Library,
where there is No Escape

Our seed library, as advertised on TikTok,
Will allow you to grow a very loving, sweet, dedicated
Obsession with difference. It will not only grow, but it will also fester
Like a disease, an addiction leading you to all kinds of automated
Error messages. It can be hard to acknowledge
That we own the rights to your very soul.
Once you trust in us, we can arrest you at any time.
Even at the news of your passing, we will not feel sad.
You may think going to the library is a nice, short, quick escape,
But we house new critters in our eaves,
Embrace coruscating satirical illustrations and
Take no prisoners. Only 90% of people can traditionally
Tell you how smart they are and our songs of willow frost
Will lull you into buying every online course you can afford and more.
Reading, after all, really is a moral action, one you must boast about.

Melting Down

March 31, 2022

If you're unfamiliar with Wisconsin geography,
Know we're all alcoholics here, drowning in lakes
Filled to the brim with booze.
When we clean our houses, we vacuum our dogs,
Eliminate pet hair from the source.
We won't apologize for calling you by the wrong name
Unless you slap us for it.
No one would accuse us of being busy working professionals,
Every hour we work is just a countdown to 5 p.m.

On a lazy Wednesday afternoon,
I continued to meet the Price family, reading memes and pretending
I had finally finished a project.
The Oscar's red carpet is filled with scandal,
Like a sudden character's death, read and re-read to make sure.
I can only concentrate on young adult novels, like a journalist
With a few screws loose.

When I was ten, I learned bad habits from a legend,
Wrote the books I couldn't find, experienced the Mandala effect,
And had the experience, values, and leadership necessary to brew
Bountiful blossoms, melting down my medals to make art.

Fitting the Mold

June 27, 2022

I stand in line for things I don't need
Never realizing I'm hungry for choice.

Instead, I create stories that serve me,
Care about appealing things, nothing too gritty.
When I vote, I follow the status quo.
I might try to pop pimples, but I won't rock the boat.

I keep my children close, their ideas closer,
Teach them how interactive fiction becomes fact,
Stuff their heads in charcoal bags so they can breathe.

When you see that all views are equally valid,
The American Taliban will take effect.

I never lost my brother to a gunman.
He was a dirty hippy, a plant parent,
Supposedly healthier homegrown.

My children and I fit the mold,
Crafted by God's intelligent design.

Ready for a Rest

July 9, 2022

Years ago, I played ukulele, my hands too small for a guitar.
I dreamed of marrying wealth, becoming a princess bride
Instead of a menopausal, middle-aged burden.

These days, I laugh at my stretch marks, the silver stripes I've earned,
The body I've built by eating, living, breeding.
I wish I could rob the riches needed for cosmetic surgery.

Suddenly, 1992 is thirty years ago, and since then,
My relationships have shifted tectonically, no one stalks my DMs,
Offering a hallucinatory escape from my life.

I hope my poetic tendencies will keep me pretty, even in death,
Teach me humility when I write the synopsis of my autobiography.
I haven't started writing it yet, but Bilbo didn't write until his hundreds.

The difference is that I might be dead by then, gone and buried.
Each chopped cord of madrone reminds me my winter is coming,
But I'm tired of life not killing me, only making me stronger.

I am ready for a rest, a decade at least of sleep.

Dreaming Fearlessly

July 10, 2022

My wife dramatically makes a difference by telling the truth.
In the five years we've been together, I've watched the days
Unfold, and never once has she played gatekeeper
To her woman magic.

As an art student, she never learned to adult,
Kept a steady relationship with chaos,
Climbed mountains and celebrated fantastical moments.

My favorite things about her are the things she tries to hide,
The darkness under her smile,
Her struggle inspires me, even as we bask in 85-degree heat.

Never once have I considered her hysterical
Or less than or weaker than me.
Today and tomorrow, she and I
Will continue to dream fearlessly.

Nothing You Do

July 11, 2022

You guys follow proven steps to prove your pride
During normal business hours, but for a limited time,
House slippers were the norm de rigueur.

You're not used to so much people-ing
Cannot connect beyond a one-night stand or random hookup.
Ignore your phone calls; send them all to voicemail.
You need to learn a new language,
Clean out the vacant spaces in your brains.

Three years ago, you would heed my recommendations,
Spend more time at the library than on TikTok
Warm your hearts in foil over coals before throwing the first brick.

I try to remember what 18 felt like, but it feels so far away
I can barely catch the thread of it, I have forgotten
What it felt like to struggle and grow.

This is where I am, trying to offer advice
When you, my students, are still my favorite artists,
Have all-access to your mindsets,
And nothing you do could upset that.

Struggling to Survive

July 12, 2022

Trapped in a room, wearing corporate logos,
I fell into a fairy tale with no happy ending.
Even my church owned me and determined my mood
So I threw a private pity party.

I survived on a fantasy, imagining I had not been taken
Advantage, that I could escape in an 800-page novel,
Combat my abusive partner's anger
By visiting London, making a movo,
Aging out of needing attention, equally valid feelings.

I painted the walls, filled the room with my worldly treasures,
But he still stood taller than me, and I took the least
Flattering selfies and eventually
Ran out of tacos to eat.

I became a burned-out meat stick, and when life
Finally started to get better, sadness overwhelmed me,
Imagining all the things I missed out on
While I struggled to survive.

Enjoy Today

We talk about "the clock app"
Fully intending to read all the books we've ever bought
And present our first US solo exhibition
Just in time to become heartstoppers.

We purify ourselves in the waters of Lake Minnetonka,
Spoiling what men had once desired, relief from
Scotland's expectations.
Our fresh faces result in shifted living arrangements,
Entire grocery aisles cater to our needs,
The picture of a perfect parking lot.

The revolution will be posted like a spoiler in a foreign language
Left like a small ball of fur, snipped from a full-page ad.
We love crocodiles, trap them for four months in pits of
Smooth recyclables, create a great opportunity.

Let's enjoy today while it's still here,
Boring and expected.

Magnificent Humans

August 19, 2022

Fuck you, hoes, I'm gonna start eating healthy,
Start reading professional-quality books,
Converting digital paintings into more traditional works.

When Christians claim they are being oppressed,
They think that they're "helping," and that they'll get an
Early bird discount on Heaven, but they know nothing.
Our love will last forever and ever, waiting for our own
Book festival, a paradise of local artists and businesses.
We'll worship Anakin Skywalker and Bob's Burgers,
Grilling up some goodness with a morning view.

When it's time to get ready for work,
I look up at the huge ball of fire emitting deadly radiation.
Blind myself like the best kind of poet,
Dream of a thousand cats.
After all, we are two magnificent humans
Who did not plan to wear the same shirt today.

Swiping Right

August 20, 2022

Hey everybody, remember to water your websites regularly,
Look how blue the water is, how wet.
Drag yourself to work, and stop carrying anger with you.
Every day is recommended for a reason,
Every big day wheezing the juice.

Before Kim K, there was Go Daddy,
There was micro-dosing.
Once you've achieved all your life goals, the circus will go on,
Marking every turquoise crone, accepting nothing less.

Find an easier way to take a snow day, to get your nails trimmed,
To absorb horror movies.
Swiftly swipe right and wish yourself a good morning.

You'll Never Make a Difference

August 22, 2022

Have you seen a $7 raise lately? Serious question.
Would you rather cha cha for charity?
How different would your life be if you could
Craft your own story from the best things you've learned?
Pass out on a fainting couch, cracking up at your mistakes?
Home is the nicest word there is,
Sleeping next to my friend, performing comedic entertainment,
Falling in love all over again.

The only measurement that matters is how much you sob,
How often you feel optimistic when you solemnly swear.
Time to grill up these weasels, suds up with peppermint body wash,
Record a video alternative to exercise.
I stand in the shower,
Waiting for a huge nerd boner,
Trying to determine where to start and end.

I am the result of a vague prayer, two adults who met
Out in the woods, selling April cauliflower.
If you're not keeping up with the weight of bees
You'll never make a difference, even if you make almost as much
Oxygen as the trees.

The Same Place

August 23, 2022

I am sorry, but I just don't think people know anything
About vaulting, about when to wake up.
Twins watch TikTok, restocking lines of poetry
Before picturing Greek gods portrayed unflatteringly.

My first novel, a journal/planner hybrid, embraces
The harshness of reality, takes you on a ghost tour,
Kills fresh in the afternoon.
The next season is already underway and
We need to ban more books immediately,
Become kings who build, launch, update, and sell
Happy birthday frequencies.
We need spelling lessons but refuse to breed.

Poets share their words, artists their paintings,
Hang out with creative contemporaries
Hoping to grow tails or other extraordinary
Limbs of note. We take the drudgery
Out of finding enlightenment, wander on
Our paths leading to the same place.

Still Breathing

August 26, 2022

Here is your constant reminder that you are still alive
But the deadline for your life is coming up fast.
You've been practicing your dance moves,
Becoming a wondrous witch,
But the DIY project that is your life could be ending soon.

Even the highest mountain knows the vacuum of space
Stretches high above it.
Sometimes words are a little too versatile,
More convenient than looking back at the 1950s
For inspiration. I saw the moon touch the earth today.
I heard the global economy can no longer afford us.

I can't believe we came here, not knowing
How compelling our story would become,
How mad we would get,
How little we would respect plants in the wild.
I grew a sunflower taller than my house,
Ventured out to the lake and forgot about the
Jaw-dropping graphics of a virtual world.

I'm just here, still breathing, on this
Beautiful summer morning.

Just As Worthy

September 6, 2022

My doubts grow louder as I near the deadline,
Can no longer subscribe to all that back-to-work mentality.
I much prefer silent quitting, doing only what is expected of me.

Today I read books instead; no labor on this Labor Day weekend,
Extended to Tuesday, no less. Instead, I did a thing,
Let my plants grow unburdened.

Brady had his loans forgiven, but I think I'm ready for a drink,
Call it a night. Let an AI write for me instead
While my liberal body sucks on paper straws.

Shout-out to the typos who survive three rounds of edits,
The genuine comfort of letting your feet be naked.
I schedule my crying and prepare for the release.

Every time someone tells me they don't read, I wonder
What advice I can give them. Remind them it isn't about speed,
That listening to audiobooks is just as worthy.

With the Addition of Food

October 9, 2022

When I took today's morning selfie, I fell in love a little bit,
With myself, finally awake, taking too much time
To count each wrinkle and fine line, each folding roll,
Each ache in my spine.

I can eat extra mozzarella sticks but
Can't find the right words and can't speak without typos.
This gift, this tater tot casserole, made by my wife
Solves all my issues. When I was a kid,
I slid on socks around the kitchen but never cooked anything.

Every social situation should include lunch,
Should be distracted by eating, should be accommodating.
Focusing on anything, without the addition of food,
Without burgers and tater tots, proves too aggravating.

Today, juggling groceries paycheck to paycheck,
I'd rather just buy what I want to eat.
My next post will be about the squid game, midnight mass,
About eating the Holy Body and enjoying unleavened bread
Spread with Holy Cheese.

Drawing of a Woman (Ink on Canvas)

October 16, 2022

My favorite drawing showcases a writer who just wants to write,
Thinking about no one, intimidating only herself,
The blank page smiling up at her, smirking.

She takes better care of herself when she takes her meds,
When her hormones are regulated, everything is controlled,
Measured, like absolute heaven, without that chaotic adrenaline.
The newest limited-edition dress with pockets fits her perfectly.
It makes her so comfortable she doesn't need to fake it,
Can sit like a fully-formed human being without crossing her legs,
Without spraining her ankles in too-high heels.

Even before her first birthday, they expected so much of her,
Expected her to blossom, to be beautiful,
To fix herself for their viewing pleasure. Now she goes
To the beauty salon just once a year to trim things,
To wax her overgrown eyebrows and faint upper lip,
But she has never kept up with it, that or shaving her legs,
Her armpits, any private places besides.
She can't "keep house" either; the dishes, the laundry,
The vacuuming. The best she can manage is wiping down the toilet,
The shower on occasion because she can't handle mold.

Last weekend, she went apple picking, felt closer to nature,
Analog in a world of technology. It felt easier, more reasonable
Than selecting produce at the grocery store, promising

She still loves her family, though she hasn't spoken to them in years,
Ignores their phone calls even. She prefers to eat alone,
Even on holidays, Christmas, Thanksgiving, Easter. Doesn't relish anything
About green bean casserole or honey-glazed ham.
For years, she worked retail, embraced the routine,
Every holiday, she got so used to it that she can't shake that expectation,
To never be around when others needed her,
Never celebrate with a significant other, or with family.
It was an incredibly convenient excuse.

Now she pulls some sleeves over her
Dress, wearing a thin jacket so she can sit on her back porch and think,
Hand poised over paper, fingers gripping a pen,
And she sighs, and she stares out of the drawing,
At whoever is watching, staring at me,
Like I rudely interrupted her brooding,
But she doesn't care to know me.
These are just the words that won't come easily,
That wrestle tumbled roughly through her mind.

Hoping for Better

October 18, 2022

I witnessed a fight-for-your-life drill:
My students cower in corners, first silent,
Then whispering, laughing, trying to pretend
None of this could happen, not here, not now,
Not to them.

They've already learned love isn't enough,
Driving cross-country, windows down in summer breeze.
It might feel good, it might make Taylor Swift an anthem.
It might count as an adventure, a joke,
But not this.

Today, I feel heavy and burdened, and I
Wish these kids could bloom like daffodils, petals flapping,
Knowing when I turn my back,
They'll still wave in the wind for a moment longer,
Won't droop or need counseling to stand upright.

This morning, I combed my fingers through my hair,
Threw it up in a sloppy ponytail, soft but insubstantial,
Feeling like a caricature of a responsible adult.
How do they expect me to shelter them,
To keep them safe when I, too, am vulnerable,
Am weak, am a phantom?

The only way to solve the world's problems
Is to come together to build the walls we need
To protect ourselves, to breathe,

To look past each moment
Into the next scene,

And hope it is better than this one.

Struggling Against Genetics

October 22, 2022

The other day, any day before today,
I honed my art, stuffed my heart
In an empty dog crate, and ate
My fear of drowning.
You taught me to swim once,
Or tried to, walking out on the beach,
Following only as far as you dared,
As I twisted myself in seaweed,
Got caught up in the waves.

I used to love the view from my bedroom,
Now all I see is your face,
Staring back at me, the age I've grown into.
If you're wondering, I spoke with my manager,
Prepared to ask for a raise,
Everything you say I deserve,
Each penny is previewed and calculated.

Each Mother's Day, I shop the clearance rack,
Waste my wishes on the hope you'll remember
My birthday this year, that you'll see me
As more than an echo.

Women often wonder if they can escape their mothers.
The answer is not in a million years,
Not when she held your hands, helping you stand

Totter forward for the first time,
Not when you forgot your locker combination,
Survived a miscarriage, then divorce.

I used to feel so graceful, so majestic,
Grasping a barre in my tutu,
Not knowing how uncertain,
How like a doll I looked in our family portrait,
How I would wear your eyes in my face.
How my smile looks just like yours,
How genetics won't let me forget,

I am your daughter and always will be,
No matter how much I struggle
Against you, and you against me.

Happy in Your Ignorance

October 23, 2022

Encourage yourselves, Wisconsin,
Beat the 2-4 team,
Hug your uncle whose chest hair
Reminds you of a mama bear,
And wear coats under your costume.
Halloween will bring snow this year,
And Christmas, a muddy jump puddle
For your newest puppy.

It's never too late for a little color
In your cheeks, a bad apple cider,
Or pumpkin beer,
Can't look away from flies
Congregating like the latest fitness craze
Was digging maggots from your trash.

If you dye your hair,
You should gaze at your grays,
Try for versatile aging, 40 years
Should be long enough to accomplish
What takes most men only 30 seconds.
Sometimes I forget,
You were born to grumble,
To argue over your son or daughter's
Gender identity at the bar,
To waste your heart on politics.

You've never needed caller ID

More than this past weekend
When the family wants to share
All the things you don't want to hear.
Surround yourself with nodders,
Those who always agree,
Regardless of what you say.
They prefer you drunk,
Using less than half your brain,
Dumb, but happy in your ignorance.

We Believe in Amen

Grassroots Open Mic

October 26, 2022

We keep Aaron Lundquist's memory alive,
Finding complexity in the simplicity of our lives,
Our souls are ready to shine.
We save for the cover charge of our afterlives,
Finding the Divine Feminine, taking her teachings,
Our morning hearts mourning the night,
Trusting the covenant, the very human agreement between us.
This collaborative inspiration sprayed with marshmallow fluff,
This little bit of pathetic poetry is just too much.
We walk through a city of roots that grew too deep -
Just remember: art is everything.

Our fingerprints come from the first prince coronated,
The translucent amber of our dreams,
These mispronounced cacophonies,
The culture that worships stupidity.
Our brains have an infestation, a manifestation
Of indescribable scribbles.
Our authentic benevolence forgives this distressing mess,
Acknowledges Woody Guthrie's influence,
Holding hands of every hue.
We'd each rather be a hippy than a railroad man,
Wish we all had kazoos.

We miss the old times, but not the old ways.
No matter how old we've grown, we have each been

The youngest person in the world, holding each premature baby,
Each handful of screaming need.
Keep love in your heart; we sing,
Too proud to beg, too dumb to steal.

We are the most dopest,
Colliding with the sunrise, full of feathered swell,
Stuck in our holy flow.
We squander our palms, spill into existence,
Where the laureates gather to blossom.
We are known and unknown, all in one breath.
From our triple great-grandmothers, we descend.
We unfurl purple petals, each crocus written eternally,
But colorfully ignored.

It shouldn't be conditional, this love.
We hold onto these temporal mementos,
And continue to build our word cred.
We have to do and be better.

Amen.

Possessive Normality

November 5, 2022

Plasma miasma browses through my furniture,
Searching for every last crumb, every moment to come.
I develop hobbies like late-night novel writing,
Failing to wake up, driving alone.
High school never haunted me; it just felt like a dream,
A singular strain of unrequited love for blue-eyed
Bank robbers, good vibes caught in the haze of Halloween,
Dirty sheets strangling my feet.
How do you stop Canadian bacon from curling?
Try polite apostrophes sprinkled like possessive normality
And grin with sharpened teeth.

You Are Better than This

November 6, 2022

Classic lemon curd tarts round out this expert ramen dinner
After we unclog the bathtub, we howl at our insecurities at 3 a.m.
If this were true, it would be oh-so-funny, so inspired –
We need giggles like we need books stacked up on the bedside table,
Whispering to us like that cupboard full of cups we never drink from.
I want to invent a new perfume that reminds me being alone isn't
A burden, just a memory, a message upon graduation:
"You are better than this, than these obsessions."

Considering Time

A popular dress arrived, shredded and torn, cute in how forlorn
And weird it seemed when I tried to wear it, when
Christmas came too early, like every year,
November and Thanksgiving were entirely forgotten.
I welcome what is logical. I subscribe to good omens,
Keeping secrets hidden, squirreling away my possessions.
My husband introduced me to my self-worth.
Before then, I was a knotted ball of anxiety,
Unable to read clocks or consider time.

Struggling to Understand Dispatch

November 6, 2022

All the truck drivers who blow their horns have nothing
Better to do, no hard realities, no broken English,
Struggling to understand dispatch. They buy gifts
For each other, slip them under the seat,
Until one finds a razor in his ass
And realizes he's been beat.

Traveling Partner at the
End of the Road

November 9, 2022

Goodbye, my beautiful boy,
With your slashed tires and broken soul.
You always listened to my every whim,
Carried me where I needed to go.
I know you will miss my rants, the way I stayed,
Doors closed, windows up, thrumming out a beat
On your steering wheel, scrolling through my phone,
Recording videos when I was already home.

You kept me warm when I wore only leggings,
When I spilled coffee into your crevices,
All the magical places we roamed.
Only time could extinguish our high-quality content,
Your box is full of condoms, used underwear, and medications.
If I were a braver person, or maybe a more scared one,
I would have hidden a handgun like a random afterthought
In that all-purpose cubby hole.
But after all these wonderful days of coaching,
Time is running out for us,
And you must return to the elements from which you came,
Your component parts, while I find a new
Traveling partner or source of conveyance.

This is the end of the road for us.

Elusive

November 10, 2022

A woman's hand is unlike a flower
Doesn't fall in love with a bee's dance
Forever sharing its swoon, deep-diving
Into stamen, piston, and pearl-pink petals.

A woman's sex is unlike a cat,
Circulating the edge of the kitchen,
Countertop to countertop throughout the day,
Mowling for attontion.

A woman's mind is unlike telepathy,
Understanding the rest of humanity,
Performing in a giant dome theatre
Then celebrating peanuts at the parade.

Instead, she draws a photo-realistic food web,
Throws herself in a tiger pit, complaining
She hasn't eaten in a long time.
Her migraine headaches wane to one per day
And she sticks to modest snacking.

The entrances and exits to her secrets become elusive.

Be Willing to Change

November 10, 2022

If you are a grown-ass man up under a woman's skirt,
You deserve who you've become, ruined.
Tailor yourself to more mature women
And maybe tonight you'll be able to express emotions.
What's the difference between this expediency
And adopting a slow work mindset?

Do you think tangerines will help you win the debate,
That one hour of sunlight will normalize
Your hero's journey?

Don't be afraid now, just be willing to change.

Feeling Better

November 16, 2022

Some of my friends don't value religion,
Won't consider their afterlife options.
An old Minnesota proverb says
A pair of scissors cut the cheese over the weekend.
But when I went to a casting event,
I didn't know what to do.
I want my social media account to be governed
By other users, the things I post in public.
I've never seen this before, so many empty spaces,
High in the guilt of cultural impact,
Overfilling the washing machine at the
Midpoint of media literacy week.
I pretend to look cute, forced to protect myself
In this interesting experiment called living as a woman.
I am constantly amazed at white out,
With how useless it is in this newest theatrical endeavor.
Finally, my bills are washed, my laundry is paid,
And I can start feeling better.

Earning Her Forgiveness

November 16, 2022

For Brandi

She dirtied her nose
Cleaning up the garden,
Snapping photos of the next generation
Of daughters valuing inner beauty,
Capturing one of the greatest memories
A day too late.

You can't compare a mother's love
To a snowball fight or a text
Coming through in the shape of a knife.
He changed her life with a sorting hat,
Shaming her motherhood,
Her playing.
Now he has grown so much; her son,
Even went trick-or-treating.

No matter how busy the Donny monster gets,
How cute, how happy,
He will always be her best pumpkin,
A little batty.
No matter how old,
His obedience training will never
Go too far for him to
Chug down a detox drink
And earn her forgiveness.

The Day You Were Absent

November 28, 2022

We cut our bangs, clapped our hands for the poets
Who hate writing but love having written.
We loved our ugly sisters, fantasized about the next two years,
Eating burgers and ribs with our fingers.
We remembered Scotland and Lord Pretty Gal,
Relaxed in a cave with goblins, naming each one Garlic or Sebastian.
We became renowned for our massive amounts of intelligence,
Ate lemon curd tarts and walked backward.
We sang in harmony, unfolded dog-eared pages,
Claimed our Irish ancestry. None of us could stop talking.
We began to tell the difference between a chemist and a plumber,
We drew cartoons of students reading and went to the bathroom outside.
We learned to change a tire and give doctors a hard time.
We went to therapy and yelled softly and napped all morning
And missed you most of all and wished you were there.

Hard Art

Grassroots Open Mic

November 23, 2022

We're all a bunch of dust
Gazing at our belly button lint.
We walk off into a gap in our minds.
We will never really ever be done
Keening and moaning to articulate
The whole of human existence.

The construction on Highway 50
Emerges more complete than our dreams,
Building a geothermal world with
A lack of analogy, the feeling of healing.
We strive to look alive, attend this church,
Is that not why we congregate?

Don't be fooled by our outer shells.
We sew the suits, but it is you who fill the costume,
And even as you grow, we know the baby will never replace you.
Yet, we are horrified by your defiance.
Now you hardly ever crawl at all,
Though you often wonder if you're a mistake.
The rain drops indiscriminately on our collective brains.

We are the biggest fighters, the poets, the writers,
A whole wide variety of hard art.
Grassroots is where we start
Building families, growing neighborhoods.

We'll always be the old souls,
Recognizing how important we each can be,
Reading more about Mr. Rodgers, but only
After the applause tapers off.

Each Part of Our Identities

December 3, 2022

Working miracles is part of living
Of loving your friends, building neural networks
Sturdy as bones, as muscle.
We need to grow stronger than our discomfort,
To reach for the next bowl of chili
While wearing our Walmart sweaters,
To dance like professional clowns.

While we live here, we hate this place,
But later, we will relate the way Die Hard
Counts as a Christmas movie, and everyone who came
To the party last week loves singing Disney karaoke.
We can only get worse and start worshipping goddesses instead.

I once witnessed a man dropping his string cheese,
Sad and melancholy, like that loss became
Suddenly tremendous, his worth wrapped in each missed bite.
We play foosball and recite sweary affirmations,
Constantly struggling with current events.

Our ADHD time blindness helps us embrace this moment,
To forget all the hate in the world.
We are working miracles here, just surviving.
Just continuing to live,
Each part of our identities proudly unfurled.

It's Not So Bad

December 5, 2022

Here's your holiday reminder:
You are not obligated to bake six dozen cookies,
Complete inane word searches or serve on a jury.

This is one of my favorite quotes:
You give me chills in your Iron Man sherpa hoodie,
Looking so cozy, so wholesome, and heartwarming.

Merry Christmas, Frank, I hope all is well.
I hope you have assembled your top ten albums of 2022,
Made friends with a mighty bear wearing a uniform, powder blue.

This library in the Netherlands lets you
Scream bloody murder down a well,
As your hormones fluctuate and everything is on sale.

I am still learning how to sleep on an Alaskan King Bed.
It's not so bad if you just let the hot sauce
Eat your flesh and then scrub it with the finest soap.

To Be Their Best Selves

December 2, 2022

Gandalf lied. He was no wizard.
He was a scribe, scrawling 700 thousand pages,
Welcoming substance into the Shire.

Curiously, he insisted on a top sheet,
Teachers and leaders no longer overburdened
By responsibilities, allowed to breathe, allowed to
Prep and grade and shut their brains away
At the end of each day.

He advocated for affordable healthcare,
For Sunday morning breakfast clubs, for recording humorous videos
Hiding underlying activism and honesty.
He found catharsis in giving away his valuables,
Held onto each bauble for no longer than a few days,
Winning trust in slow motion.

He auditioned for Santa Clause but couldn't properly
Lie to the children, couldn't listen to one more rendition
Of Jingle bells on an out-of-tune xylophone.

He took to telling puns instead,
Sharing bountiful groans with friends,
And they would always welcome him,
If sometimes begrudgingly, knowing what he would ask of them:
To be their best selves, in the best ways, always.

I'll Survive Just the Same

December 6, 2022

Phone numbers give me the creeps.
Why would anyone need to reach me,
Need to insert themselves into my hand, my ear,
To be so near to me?
My skin is not soft, not supple, and buttery,
I don't believe in kindness or small talk, or flattery.
You'd need to wave an oversized, all-caps, obnoxious
Banner at me to prove that you're flirting.

I just don't see the point in trying.
I'd rather eat my chips and queso alone.
I am addicted to my antisocial notoriety.
Teach only because it gives me an opportunity
To nerd out to people who are forced to listen to me.
It's Tuesday, but here I am recording,
Watching out for things better left unsaid.

But I'll think them anyway, spread each thought
Like love was thin jelly on toast,
Like space dust is my home décor
And tarot tells the truth.
Art is making a thing and then trying to make a better one
Until your remaining hobbies become commodified
And your fans become obsessed with the way
You ended that last line without a rhyme
And your rhythm goes wonky.

Time off from social activities would do me good,

It would teach me to meet myself, to face infinity.
Instead, I waste my free time counting likes and follows
And trending innovations breed uncertainty.

One day, it will hit me,
And I'll be able to define what it is,
Or maybe I'll just curl up and read
Someone else's thoughts, abandon
All hope of poetic fame.
But I'll survive just the same.

Everything is Somehow
Still Okay

December 7, 2022

AI art isn't art, it is a travesty,
Trying to take the place of humanity,
No matter what else you put on your to-do list
Include this: disrupt hegemony, the status quo,
Support real artists and their craft but realize
In the end, there are no rules.

No matter what the teacher says, someone in homeroom
Will still snort lemonade powder at a friend's suggestion.
I may or may not have been that friend –
The one with the great but dangerous ideas,
But you put the rain in brainwash,
Put the cycle through another rinse.

Despite this, self-expression is always in style,
Every step we take outside our comfort zones.
The kids say they want less overwhelm,
But I feel called out on Human Rights Day.
What rights have we each had taken away,
Hour by hour, inch by inch, our safe spaces
Growing ever smaller? The perimeter of our permissions
Drawn tighter and tighter, the places
Where we can still peacefully coexist?

The Holy Chao of Eris welcomes winter babies,
Sleeping out in the snow,

Connecting each heart and soul through a For You page.
Yet, we all want the look everyone is talking about,
The confetti in our screams, the glitter in our tears,
To pretend everything is somehow
Still okay.

All of Us Are Worthy

Grassroots Open Mic

December 14, 2022

This morning knows nothing of my dreams,
My attempts to make sense of it all.
I have a heart here for the whole world to hold
Each piece is chopped bite-size for you freaks.

Let me throw down the fruits of my vocabulary,
My voice was never silenced.
I will sing to my bones,
Un-squandering my wandering perspective,
As true as your own emotions.

Today was a happy day, offset by what moved me,
What made me feel unreal.
I am here to stay, dropping bombs of bourbon
As my knees want to buckle,
My lungs breathe greedily.
Everything I was, I despise.
This is how flesh disappears, superficial skin,
A little taste of catastrophe.

But I want you to listen intently.
Don't get too comfortable in your comfort.
Right at the cusp of winter, some celebrate the darkest night,
Here in spirit always.
They embrace poetic phrasing, sound it out,
Echo every hope we hold for ourselves.

Living on in our memories,
Each time we repeat their names in this
Suddenly sacred space.

Give yourself a moment, let it breathe,
Let it feed your soul and know,
In the end, all of us are worthy.

Eventually

December 25, 2022

Grandma's crooked curlicues,
Ragged names and "I love you"
Lost to a digital generation
Rapt with lol emojis

It's not that they can't communicate
They do – always chattering away,
Always sending off texts, electronic messages,
But their eyes hesitate
Fall heavy on looped letters

Like images black-and-white,
Stone-faced portraits from another time,
Or, further still, etched tablets, cave scratches
We can still observe humanity,
But can no longer read
We no longer understand what they mean

Grandma's arthritic hands
Can no longer look forward to a legible response
Handwritten in ink
Her time has come and gone

As will this generation's -
Eventually

Learning Patience

December 27, 2022

Cookies and crime go hand-in-hand with mahogany mommies
Sweet-sounding turns of phrase are not meant to break your brain
But sound and claim meaning by grasping at
Lowest hanging fruit, almost cliché, too good to be true.

I'm sorry I had to make you a villain in my story,
It was the only way I could still be the protagonist,
Could justify my bad behavior without footnotes, addendums,
Unwieldy backstory. Truth is, I'm exhausted.

When we converted 4000 into Roman numerals,
The result was a low hum, thrumming through the fridge,
But not keeping the beer cold enough.
I made an acute snow angle today – that was not a typo,
That was the truth; longer than my 2023 reading list,
The backlog of my bookcase weighed in unused screws,
Maybe one was loose.

Bukowski's beer-drunk soul was sadder than
All the dead Christmas trees of the world,
Sacrificing their greenery for a few weeks of merriment.
Despite everything, sorry is always in season,
Delivering tears for anyone missing
Loved ones, a cat frozen to the sidewalk.

We don't have the tools to cope
With dental office receptionists, the hold line
For unemployment, the trauma we have inherited.

At thirty, my parents worried about less
Inconsequential ideas, like struggling to tame me.
I love your dad jokes, their wholesome, painfully
Obvious quality, like top hats, never quite out of style.

Why did you leave, then, in this freezing weather,
When you knew I planned to knit you
A warmer scarf, if you could just be patient,
Maybe even a sweater?

Like Cranberry Juice

December 28, 2022

I will give a prize to the first person
Willing to be my family,
But it might be a white elephant Christmas gift.
Where are my bookworms? You are welcome already.
Enjoy a sneak peek into my mental wanderings.

How many holidays do you celebrate?
I want them all, even the most obscure ones,
And a union that will allow paid time off for them.
Caught in fairy tale side quests, I file my feels away,
Grasp onto the more glamorous parts of my job.

Today, my existence is brought to you by
Witchy grab bags, Tik Tokkers ready to tell off bullies.
We are making our own family.
You are my sister, my brother, my child, my parent,
My long lost aunt from Kentucky because you recognize
Just how frustrating sensory overload can be
How I grow paralyzed on a 10-hour Netflix binge –
Show me how well you know me
By knowing yourself, my friend,
Realizing it might not work out in the end.

We might lose touch, you might move across the country,
But when you call, when you visit,
It will be like no time has passed, and our friendship
Picks right back up, we join in accomplishing each pointless task.
Disclaimer: It's easier with more hands, but just in case

I told everyone we're hibernating so we can ignore deadlines,
Finish our least favorite chores last.

I want to pet every fuzzy thing, so we should visit
The shelter this afternoon, I want to adopt every puppy
If just for a moment, embrace our geek culture and artifacts.
Sometime in the future, they will call this a movement,
The way we dance, trying desperately to invoke serotonin,
To start our own YouTube channels, to avoid your ex.
Just shoveling out the drive is a conspiracy theory,
An unnecessary task if we stay cuddled in our blanket fort.

My foundation is weak, cheap, can't stand up on my own,
My Halloween costume is just always me,
Wearing too much makeup, just let everyone know
They're welcome here – it isn't a limited-time offer.
I mean it when I call you family –
Just like cranberry juice, I go with everything.

ACKNOWLEDGEMENTS

The author would like to acknowledge the following individuals:

Nick Ramsey for always inviting me to Grassroots Open Mic, even when I can't make it. The lyrics and lines of other artists inspire several of the poems in this collection.

Donovan Scherer at Studio Moonfall and Samantha (Sam) Jacquest at Blue House Books for supporting me and selling my books to the locals.

My friends on social media, whose statuses I have borrowed from, and who also support my publishing adventures.

My family who have always been supportive, if not always understanding, of my poetry.

Kaitlyn Bolyard teaches writing and literature at DePaul University and Carthage College. She lives in Wisconsin with her chef husband, who keeps her well-fed. She writes mostly poetry because it can be finished in one sitting, but she has also started writing novels as well. You can visit her at kaitlynbolyard.com.

Also by Kaitlyn Bolyard

Echoing Back at You: A Decade of Social Media Poetry

Kaitlyn Bolyard uses social media statuses as the fodder for her poetry, often with strange and hilarious results. Some of her most recent poems have even taken on a more insightful tone, allowing readers to look into what is happening in the world and how it affects our day-to-day lives. For the past decade (2011-2021), she has been crafting these poems, posting them on social media, borrowing from friends' statuses, writing for friends, and sharing at open mics.